WINTER

Mon pays ce n'est pas un pays, c'est l'hiver,
Mon jardin ce n'est pas un jardin, c'est la plaine,
Mon chemin ce n'est pas un chemin, c'est la neige,
Mon pays ce n'est pas un pays, c'est l'hiver.

My country's not a country, it's winter,
My garden's not a garden, it's the plains,
My road's not a road, it's the snow,
My country's not a country, it's winter.

GILLES VIGNEAULT

'Winter! from thy crystal throne,
With a keenness all thy own
Dartest thou, through gleaming air,
O'er the glorious barren glare
Of thy sunlit wilderness

CHARLES G. D. ROBERTS

THE WINTER PRAIRIE, NEAR BRANDON, MANITOBA

Winter is the season of the return to the infinite, to the incomplete that is man.... It is also the season of the return from the infinite in the Christian mystery of God made into man. Return to, return from: these two expressions mean basically the meeting between the infinite which is in God and the infinite which is in man and which, in the final analysis, are made to link up and touch one another.

PIERRE TROTTIER

NIAGARA FALLS IN FEBRUARY

But the light is swiftly fading,
And the wind is icy cold;
And a mist the moon is shading,
Pallid in the western gold;
In the night-winds still ye nod,
Sentinels of Nature's God.

FREDRICK GEORGE SCOTT

BLOWING SNOW ON A SASKATCHEWAN HIGHWAY

Snow—snow—fast-falling snow!
Snow on the housetops—snow on the street
Snow overhead, and snow under feet
Snow in the country—snow in the town
Silently, silently sinking down
Everywhere, everywhere, fast-falling snow,
Dazzling the eye with its crystalline glow!

JAMES P. MOFFATT

TORONTO'S OLD CITY HALL

Now soon, ah, soon, I know
The trumpets of the north will blow,
    And the great winds will come to bring
The pale wild raiders of the snow.

BLISS CARMAN

THE MAIN LINE OUT OF WINNIPEG

Never a bud of spring, never a laugh of summer,
    Never a dream of love, never a song of bird;
But only the silence and white, the shores that
    grow chiller and dumber,
Wherever the ice winds sob, and the griefs of winter
    are heard.

WILFRED CAMPBELL

A WINDBLOWN APPLE TREE , MAHONE BAY, NOVA SCOTIA

The sky has for me become one of possibilities, just as have winter, ice, and snow, which I no longer regard as burdens, prisons, or tortures, but rather as a new form of freedom.

PIERRE TROTTIER

SNOW-COVERED STUBBLE ON THE SASKATCHEWAN PRAIRIE

Canada grows out of its deeps now
and the snow burns off in the glow
and the snow is make-believe on the vast stretches
       between
but make-believe enough to fill a child of the past
       with shivers and cold love
passing at night over the rail that may leave no track
through the wooded and white land of the broken
       birch
and pine and spruce locked down and the quietness
sheeting by peculiarly to itself yet lasting so long
that it is there travelling too, a ghostly companion.

DOROTHY ROBERTS

BOW RIVER, BANFF NATIONAL PARK

Winter forests mutely standing
Naked on your bed of snow,
Wide your knotted arms expanding
To the biting winds that blow,
Nought ye heed of storm or stress,
Stubborn, silent, passionless.

FREDERICK GEORGE SCOTT

SUNRISE IN MANITOBA

White are the far-off plains, and white
The fading forests grow;
The wind dies out along the height,
And denser still the snow,
A gathering weight on roof and tree,
Falls down scarce audibly.

ARCHIBALD LAMPMAN

ST-JOSEPH, NEW BRUNSWICK,
CHRISTMAS EVE

WINTER

PIERRE BERTON

PHOTOGRAPHS BY ANDRÉ GALLANT

Stoddart

Printed in Singapore

Published in 1994 by
Stoddart Publishing Co. Limited
34 Lesmill Road
Toronto, Canada
M3B 2T6
(416) 445-3333

Canadian Cataloguing in Publication Data

Berton, Pierre, 1920–
    Winter

ISBN 0-7737-2805-8

1. Winter – Canada. 2. Canada – Social life and customs. 3. Canada – Description and travel.
I. Title.

FC85.B47 1994   971   C94-930605-3
F1021.B67 1994

Stoddart Publishing gratefully acknowledges the support of the Canada Council, the Ontario Ministry of Culture, Tourism and Recreation, Ontario Arts Council, and Ontario Publishing Centre in the development of writing and publishing in Canada.

INTRODUCTION

WE CANADIANS ARE A WINTER PEOPLE—A *WINTRY* people, some would say—frosty of mien, cool of temperament, chilly of countenance. We are not given to public displays of hot emotion. We do not wear our hearts on our sleeves, as summer people do, or hold our hands over our hearts. One cannot imagine an audience in Joe Batt's Arm, Trois-Rivières, Okotoks, or Powell River fervently reciting a Pledge of Allegiance in unison.

Summer people are hot-blooded, as befits their southern climates. They jostle each other in the crowded streets as the sun beats down. But we are a closed-door people and we like to keep our distance. The sidewalk café is not part of our tradition. "December," as Alden Nowlan has written in "Canadian Love Song," "is thirteen months long, July's one afternoon. . ." The climate militates against riot and revolution. It is rare for Canadians to raise their voices in a windblown public square, and one cannot imagine a gunfight in Moose Jaw in January. How could anyone reach for a weapon concealed beneath three layers of wool and fur?

Our emotions, too, are kept tightly wrapped. Yet that does not mean that we lack passion. In "Love Where the Nights Are Long," Irving Layton points out that Canadians have written some of the best love poetry in the world because, being a "backward folk . . . they have not heard that love is dead." I doubt that we are backward. "Buoyant" is a better description, for winter has made us a buoyant people—a tough, resilient breed, able to adapt to the longest of our seasons, to come to terms with it, to survive it—yes, and to celebrate it. The stunning pictures that follow say it all.

My sister, Lucy (left)*, and I, bundled up for winter, outside our home in Dawson City,* circa *1923.*

A WINTER
CHILDHOOD

December 21, 1928, Dawson City, Yukon Territory.

My father and I are floundering through the snow, working our way up the hill behind our house, searching for the perfect Christmas tree. We move through a shadowless world, stark and eerie, devoid of colour, silent as the sepulchre. The only sound is the faint squeak of the snow, dry as sand, beneath our feet. No breath of air rattles the bony branches of the birches and aspens, which rise in their thousands out of the drifts around us, like skeletal fingers pointing towards a sullen sky.

It is the winter solstice, the darkest of the dark days, celebrated since ancient times as the moment of the sun's rebirth. Like the primitive peoples of old, we long for the day when the sun will begin to come back to us, and we celebrate that promise with garlands of coloured lights. It is no accident that the great midwinter festivals of ancient times closely surrounded Christmas, for the birth of a new year and the solstice itself have always been seen as a single event to which another birth—that of the Deity—has been appended.

Our festival of light begins with a series of Christmas parties and is climaxed by a New Year's Eve masked ball, dominated by a gigantic spruce tree aflame with electric colour, defying the winter gloom. The spruce and not the maple is the real symbol of Canada. It flourishes in 90 percent of the country, a tree designed by nature for winter, its branches sloping downward, allowing the weight of the snow to slide away before its limbs can break, and thus creating the familiar Yuletide pattern, a triangle of evergreen, counterfeited in shop windows, greeting cards, and soft drink ads.

The fog of winter hangs like a pall over the town below. The smoke from a hundred furnaces pillars upward in unwavering columns. The flat light of noon has already given way to twilight, although it is scarcely three o'clock. On the main roadways the street lamps create glowing pools in the snow. We find the tree we want in a ravine, part of a wavering smear of spruce reaching up the flanks of the hillside and contrasting sharply with the chalky trunks of the leafless aspens. Below us, as we drag our tree back down the slope, more lights wink on.

We crave the man-made light, for nature has deprived us of the sun. For six weeks it lies low, concealed behind the encircling hills. We trudge off to school in the dark, muffled to the eyes, and we trudge home in the dark, accepting grudgingly our daily spoonful of cod-liver oil in lieu of the warming rays. We look forward hungrily to that moment when the sun will peep briefly over the far hillside and cast a thin shaft onto the wooden sidewalk at the corner of Fifth Avenue and Church Street in the centre of town. We stand there, gawking at the miracle until the light winks out, comforted by the knowledge that it will return and stay longer as the January days drag on. Now for the first time in six weeks we will again be able to see our shadows.

In my childhood, winter was the dominant season, as, indeed, it is for most Canadians. Spring and fall were fleeting; summer was a short, torrid burst of endless light; but winter went on forever, or so it seemed to us. It began early in October with the first wet flakes of snow and lasted until the ice broke in the Yukon River in late April or early May.

Yet, in spite of the cold and the darkness, I cannot look back on my Yukon winters with anything but pleasure. Winter, after all, is the children's season. I find it difficult in memory to associate it with cold. Yes, I suffered from mild frostbite on my cheeks and nose, and, yes, my feet were seldom warm; but I still think of those childhood years in terms of the outdoors.

We walked half a mile to school in all temperatures, and we walked home for lunch even when the thermometer dropped as low as minus sixty degrees Fahrenheit. I have known a more numbing cold in Aldershot, England, in March 1945 than in the Yukon. As a child, I welcomed thirty-below weather as relatively mild, for at that temperature we shed our furs and switched to mackinaws. We learned to protect our noses with mufflers so that the frost could not reach our lungs, and we knew enough to keep our naked fingers—and certainly our tongues—away from exposed metal. We had

learned that the hard way when the older boys dared us to lick the doorknob! (Children are surely the cruellest animals on earth.)

The school did not close, even when the temperature reached record lows. My mother, who taught kindergarten in Dawson before the Great War, used to talk of the horror of recess. She would have to dress a dozen or more of her small charges—each wearing two pairs of socks, two pairs of mitts (tied together by long strings and pinned to their coats), double woollen tuques, and two mufflers, one tied around the waist of their coonskin coats. Out into the school yard the little tots would tumble only to return ten minutes later, when my mother would have to go through the exhausting process of removing their outer clothing, now damp with melting snow.

We older kids made angels in the snow and played hockey without skates on the hardened surface of the school yard. We pulled our tuques down over our faces and dove head first into the deep, snow-filled ditches that drained the swampy town in the spring. We went on winter hikes, building enormous fires and munching sandwiches frozen hard as ship's biscuit. We raced, belly buster, down the hills on fast sleds that hugged the ground.

We could not skate on the river, for it was a tangle of ice blocks. Nor do I recall that anyone in those days took to skis. But for Christmas I was given a pair of snowshoes as tall as I was—not the traditional bear-paw style used in the East, but long and slender, fashioned for the dry, crusted snow of the Klondike valley. On these we tramped out trails that hardened overnight and

My mother, Laura Berton, takes me for a ride through the Yukon snow with the help of our family husky, Grey Cloud. This was a relatively mild winter's day, about –20°F.

easily bore our weight, once we had mastered the shuffling glide that every snowshoer must adopt. Sometimes I would harness my husky dog, Spark (named for Barney Google's comic-strip racehorse), and persuade him to pull me, somewhat reluctantly, out along the road that bordered the banks of the frozen Klondike.

Winter began, not just with the first snow, but also with the Last Boat. There was a wan symbolism here, for the boat meant that our lifeline to the Outside world had been cut. Those who stepped aboard said goodbye to winter; those who remained on shore prepared for it. We stood on the wharf, bidding goodbye to the people of summer, leaving for warmer climes. Some, including friends of childhood, might be leaving forever. They stood at the steamboat's rail, waving sadly as the grey river bore them south. When she reached

Here I am, pulling my sister's sled along Dawson's Fifth Avenue in front of the Territorial Administration Building where my father worked. This is early winter—too early for fur coats—when the snow was soft enough to stick to clothing.

the centre of the current, the whistle sounded. As that final wail echoed across the hills, part of our community vanished beyond the Yukon's bend, leaving only a puff of white smoke to mark its passing.

The flight from winter! It takes place with more dispatch today, thanks to modern transportation, but it remains a Canadian phenomenon. In the summertime, Dawson City accommodated at least one thousand souls. When the snows came, we were reduced to about five hundred. Some had left for school or college, some to retire or die, some because there was little work in the wintertime, all because they had neither need nor desire to be frozen in for eight months in a northern ghost town. For the community wound down in winter. The big dredges, churning up the creek beds in search of the last traces of Klondike gold, ceased to operate. The steamboats went into winter quarters. Life slowed, as it did in most of Canada.

We were now isolated. To flee from Dawson required considerable fortitude once winter set in. It meant a frigid five-day ride in an open sleigh drawn by a Caterpillar tractor, bouncing along the roller-coaster road that led up the frozen river. It meant five nights sleeping in draughty roadhouses, crammed together with fellow passengers, half suffocated by the steam from wet clothes hanging over a red-hot stove. No one made that trip south on the mail stage unless it was desperately necessary.

When the first gossamer flakes drifted over the town, we children greeted them with shrieks of joy. The fresh snow packed easily, to be shaped into forts, snowmen, and miniature cannonballs. We rolled in the snow, our woollens beaded with it, our faces damp with the melt. As the skies darkened and the snow continued to fall, we helped our parents shovel it off the roofs of the cottages and cabins to prevent them from caving in. Then we took turns sliding down these roofs into the mountains of snow at the base. But when the real cold descended and the snow no longer packed, the forts, snowball fights, and sliding ended.

By November, the river was running with ice. The water rose, the current increased in speed, the ice floes grew larger, roaring and crashing, rending and tearing as they smashed against each other and piled up. The centre of the stream now resembled a gorge as the water froze outward from both shores and the masses of ice were piled high on either side. At last, almost in an instant, the freezing waters seemed to solidify, and the entire channel was clogged with massive, up-ended cakes, jammed together in a solid, unmoving mass. Across these misshapen hummocks we would be able to make our way from shore to shore on weekend outings.

Bicycles had long since been put away. Automobiles went into sheds. The town tinkled with the sound of sleigh-bells on dogs and horses. When the temperature dropped past forty below, the Mounted Police kept their horses stabled to protect their lungs from the cold. Only one motorcar remained operative—Archie Fournier's hand-cranked Model T, which brought the milk around in used brown beer bottles. Normal thermometers did not work; mercury freezes at forty below. My father was able to fashion a scarf pin out of that metal. He wore it outdoors for two weeks before it finally melted.

In the winter, we were without running water. It would have been impossible to heat the mains, except those that serviced the downtown core. The water wagon came around twice a week, and we were supplied from its tank. Two sturdy men, with icicles dripping from their moustaches, carried in two four-gallon pails made from gasoline tins and splashed them into the cistern in our kitchen. I still remember those water days, when the kitchen door was thrown open and a blast of winter entered our house in a chill fog. There was another weekly duty. The scavenger arrived with his cart and emptied the one-holer in our basement—an essential service in a community where flush toilets were unknown.

When the freeze-up came, the roar of the Klondike pouring into the Yukon River was muted, to be replaced by the screech of a portable sawmill cutting our wood into stove lengths. Like every other building in Dawson, our house was heated with birchwood. Behind the sprawling Administration Building where my father worked were long rows of cordwood, piled high, in which we children played hide-and-seek. There was no coal. Everything ran on birchwood, including the stern-wheeled steamboats. One of my winter chores was to bring it into the basement by the armful to fuel the furnace. The sawdust filled the space between the double walls, about a foot apart, of most houses, forming effective insulation. And so one of my winter memories is of suffocating heat rather than cold. In the cabins, the Yukon stoves glowed red, and the atmosphere was stifling. You burst in from the blizzard and a wall of heat struck you. There seemed to be no middle ground. You either shivered or sweated.

We learned to guess at the outside temperature from the nails that held the weather stripping to the kitchen door. The metal conducted the cold so that the nail heads became frosted in ascending order—or so we believed. My mother had another method of telling the temperature. When the thermometer dropped below minus forty, a thick fog settled over the Yukon valley. She has written that she could pretty well judge the temperature by the fog's density. If the houses a short block away were invisible, she knew it was at least forty below. If those half a block away could not be seen, it was fifty below. And if Robert Service's former cabin across the street—now a local shrine—was shrouded, she could be fairly certain that it was fully sixty below zero.

This was almost seventy years ago. More than sixty of those years have passed since I have experienced a northern winter. I live now in rural Ontario, where the season lasts no more than four months and is much more bearable than it used to be. When the maples are bled of their leaves and the garden is a black ruin, we find ourselves longing for the moment when the world turns pure. We greet the first soft flakes with jubilation, as children have always done. We exclaim in wonder as each tree takes on its coating of white, and we rush to find our cameras to record the miracle. We build snow forts and snow people. We shovel off the pond for skating parties. The squeals of tobogganing children split the chilly silence. Winter in all its beauty—yes, and all its terror—has arrived. Even as we welcome the change of season we put a snow shovel and sack of sand in the trunk of the car. Some weeks will pass before we get out the tourist brochures and seek a brief haven in the tropical sun.

TWILIGHT AT NOON

Although my old home town lies south of the Arctic Circle, the surrounding hills hide the sun for about six weeks in midwinter. People go to work and come home in the dark, with only a brief twilight break at the lunch hour. It can be very cold in Dawson. I can remember the temperature dropping past minus 60 degrees Fahrenheit. We children were taught to keep muffled up, our noses and mouths protected from icy blasts that could freeze a spot on the lungs and our ears covered to prevent the sting of frostbite.

Firewood, often hand cut, was the only fuel we knew in my day. Birch was universally used because, as a hardwood, it made hotter, more effective fires than poplar or spruce.

The legendary log cabin is making a comeback in Dawson, where many are now prefabricated out of matched logs. They even do duty as children's playhouses.

Above: *On this December morning, the sun peeks briefly over the encroaching hills to shine for the last time on the façades of the pioneer buildings, including the restored post office in the foreground. It will not return until mid-January.*

Left: *It's only mid-afternoon, but Dawson City is already enveloped by the dark shroud of winter on this chill December day. The street lights are turned off in late morning and turned back on early in the afternoon.*

Previous page: *This photograph, taken at high noon from the Midnight Dome above Dawson, shows the river, still unfrozen, winding northward on its way to the Bering Sea—some 1,500 miles away.*

The fog of winter blurs the conifers on the hills above the Roman Catholic church as the first snow of winter powders
Dawson's wooden sidewalks. Most cars now are able to operate in spite of the weather.
In my day, the Model Ts and Studebaker touring cars were stored away until spring.

On Third Avenue, new false-fronted buildings hint at an earlier, gaudier age. In summer, the Eldorado Motel is overbooked with tourists seeking to relive the gold rush days. But in winter it is virtually empty as half the population departs for warmer climes, leaving Dawson to hardier folk who share the dark season with the rugged canines.

THE IMAGE
OF WINTER

MOST OF THE ADULTS I KNOW (IN CONTRAST WITH small children) hate winter. The only thing they hate more is other people's image of Canada as a snow-covered waste. We have never quite forgiven Kipling for identifying this country as "Our Lady of the Snows," and when an American weather report refers to "a cold front coming down from Canada," we bristle. David Phillips, a Canadian government climatologist, has tried to reassure us that "most of Canada's nastiest weather. . . comes from the United States—monster snows, freezing rains, hurricanes." But that doesn't help, especially as Phillips himself has also pointed out that the only national capital colder than Ottawa is Mongolia's, that Winnipeg is the coldest city of its size on the globe, and that Montrealers shovel more snow than any other urbanites in the world. That is not an image we like to boast about. Although some government tourist brochures show happy people skiing in the Laurentians, there are far more pictures of green golf courses and limpid mountain lakes than of tourists braving the elements. It is natural enough. As Norman Pressman has explained in an essay written for the Institute of Urban Studies, "winter tends to be a season which dwellers of cold regions try vehemently to deny."

For most of our history we have done our best to pretend that a Canadian winter isn't all that miserable. Cold? William Van Horne, who built the CPR and became a Canada booster as a result, never lost an opportunity to suggest that the prairies were close to being subtropical. During one European tour he declared that the coldest weather he had ever encountered was in Rome and Florence. "I pine for Winnipeg to thaw me," he said, without so much as cracking a smile. "The atmosphere in the Far West intoxicates me, it is so invigorating." Van Horne, an expert at five-card stud, had long since developed a poker face.

"Invigorating"—that was the great buzzword used by the Canadian government to lure immigrants to the Canadian West and erase the image of Canada as a blizzard-swept desert. That required considerable ingenuity. *Blackwood's*, the Scottish periodical, had referred to it as "our frozen frontier." The *Nation* of Dublin had damned the Dominion as "a kind of Siberia." William Ewart Gladstone had said it was a country "of perpetual ice and snow." The pamphleteers of Clifford Sifton's Department of the Interior did their best to

The image of the passionate and virile Canadian was perpetuated by Hollywood silent films. This one, The Storm (opposite), *based on a Broadway play of the same name, was made in 1930. It was the third filming of the play, this time directed by William Wyler. The girl is the Mexican actress Lupe Velez.*

twist this image into an asset. "Cold" and "frost" were taboo words in the official handouts, which were studded with acceptable adjectives such as "bracing," "buoyant," and "healthful." By the end of the century, when the tide of immigrants was approaching a flood, Canadians stopped apologizing for the weather, convincing newcomers—and each other—that they were a rugged people, rendered sturdy by a climate that helped to maintain health and stimulate robustness.

The notion that climate affects character was popularized in the eighteenth century by the French philosopher Montesquieu, who wrote that "the temper of the mind and the passions of the heart are extremely different in different climates. . . ." Canada boosters of the nineteenth century subscribed to it. Charles Mair, the Canadian nationalist poet, praising the lightness, dryness, and sparkle of the Canadian winter, declared that the entire atmosphere was charged with ozone, "that element that is closely associated with soundness of mind and body." Lord Dufferin, the Governor General, claimed that "a constitution nursed upon the oxygen of our bright winter atmosphere. . .makes its owner feel as though he could toss about pine trees in his glee." The great Canadian physician William Osler predicted that in the future "the most virile nation on the continent will be to the north of the Great Lakes."

One leading Montreal surgeon even went so far as to suggest that death from cold was a pleasant experience: "The countenances of those frozen to death are singularly calm and placid, and not indicative of any suffering." He described one such death in which the victim died in an attitude of prayer, "a smile on his rigidly frozen face."

The image of Canadians as a rugged race of outdoorsmen was perpetuated by Hollywood during the first half of this century. Unfortunately, almost every movie with a Canadian theme also perpetuated another image (the very one the tourist boosters were trying to avoid), that of a land covered in impassable snows. During the silent days, Canada was rarely identified in movie titles. Instead it was referred to obliquely as the Land of the Big Snows—"the eternal snows of Northern Canada," in the phrase of one English reviewer, or "a land of measureless snows," to quote an ad for a Tom Mix Western. In the American South during midsummer, exhibitors used "snow pictures" as a kind of early day air conditioning. "PLAY THIS AND BEAT THE HEAT," one ad advised. "*Snowblind* will cool your house and make the patrons happy." Another promised "mile upon mile of banked-up snow—ice-encrusted pine trees—Arctic winds whistling through the valleys. . . ." Some enterprising U.S. exhibitors created "snow lobbies" for movies with Canadian ambiance, complete with cutout icicles and white paint sprinkled with mica. One man even built a frozen lake in the lobby. This was serious stuff. Hollywood made close to six hundred pictures with Canadian themes; only six were comedies. Four got laughs by showing Canadians shivering in the cold.

Hollywood's other cliché—the regenerative powers of the Canadian winters—fitted more neatly into the conception of the tourist industry. Desperately wounded at Waterloo, Major John Gordon is packed off to "the balsamic air of the Canadian pine forest." A few sniffs of the evergreens and he's a new man. Moral resuscitation was an even stronger story line. The cleansing effect of

Canadians of the nineteenth century liked to see themselves depicted as rugged outdoorsmen, inured to a winter climate.
But this photograph, like so many others, was created in the warmth of a photographer's studio, complete with fake snow.

the eternal snows was a plot device used to provide a virtuous climax for those films that dealt with the popular Escape from a Corrupt Society theme. "I'm going to take her away from this rotten civilization!" cries Jim Belmont, wealthy Los Angeles tycoon, as he snatches his daughter from his estranged wife. *Cut* to pine trees, snow-capped mountains, and the subtitle: "Far away in Canada—safe from the evils of civilization."

We cannot blame Hollywood, for this was exactly the image Canadians had of themselves. The winter climate, so it was claimed, had made Canadians superior to other races. Virtue and moral purity went hand in hand with a "bracing" environment. We were, in short, as pure as the driven snow. A leading Canadian educator, George Parkin, principal of Upper Canada College, subscribed to that view. A cold climate, he wrote in 1895, "tends to produce a Puritan turn of mind which gives moral strenuousness." That attitude

A rare Hollywood comedy about Canadian winter, starring the great Buster Keaton, was called, of course, The Frozen North.

extended into the new century and clearly influenced the paintings of the Group of Seven, one of whom, Lawren Harris, wrote that "our whole country is cleansed by the pristine and replenishing air that sweeps out of that great hinterland."

A leading student of the Canadian character, Carl Berger, has pointed out that, in Canadian eyes, "the adjective 'northern' came to symbolize energy, strength, self reliance, health, and purity, and its opposite, 'south-ern,' was equated with decay and effeminacy, even libertinism and disease." Racism was certainly inherent in the immigration department's policies. Southern peoples, such as Italians, weren't wanted. Blacks were kept out on the excuse that they couldn't stand the Canadian winter. Natives of cold countries—Scandinavians, Poles, Ukrainians, and Germans—were welcomed.

The idea that freedom and liberty are the concomitants of a cold climate was widely accepted. The winds of liberty, it was held, blew down from the north. After all, the anthem reminded us that we were "the True North strong and free." As one writer put it, "If climate has not had the effect of moulding races, how is it that southern nations have invariably been inferior to and subjugated by the men of the north?"

In George Parkin's belief, the cold weather acted as "a permanent barrier to the influx of weaker races." The climate alone prevented the emergence of "shiftless and improvident" tramps. Canadian cities would never know labour agitation because Canadians had been conditioned by climate to a rugged individualism, while the "grumblers" would quickly head south. Our cities would also be safe from "the gradual and inevitable spread of a black zone across the South" and from "the vagrant population of Italy and other countries of Southern Europe."

I wonder what Parkin would think today of our largest metropolis, Toronto, with its huge Italian, Portuguese, Greek, and Caribbean population. History makes clear that climate has never deterred strangers from crowding in. Since the days of the Bering land bridge, new arrivals have been braving and conquering the blasts of winter in their search for a more abundant life.

THE IMAGE REVIVED

There was a time when anyone who tried to cross the St. Lawrence in the dangerous in-between season had to be both rugged and adventurous. When the river was filled with floating ice and the paddlewheel steamers stopped running, the only way to get from Quebec City to the south shore was by canoe—not a fragile birchbark craft, but a rugged wooden one that would withstand the battering from the ice. The crews of these big winter canoes were "canotiers"— hardy French Canadians of the voyageur breed, whose image has been perpetuated in the annual canoe race across the same dangerous stretch of ice-clogged river.

Modern canotiers have to be as rugged and—some would say—as foolhardy as their eighteenth-century predecessors. The old-timers crossed the river only when it was absolutely necessary, their passengers sheathed in buffalo robes. In the old days a journey to the south shore was never made for pleasure. Today's contestants in the annual canoe race, dressed in modern ski clothes, do it for thrills and, of course, the joy of winning.

The river surface is normally three quarters ice to one quarter water. Often enough, the huge ice blocks, careering down the half-frozen river, come together to form a solid mass. The canotiers must then leap from their craft onto the treacherous, moving ice and pull or push their 250-pound canoe like a sleigh until a clear channel is reached. They use Olympic graphite oars, very light and stiff. The boats are waxed, like skis, before entering the river.

In the old days the skipper would cross himself and murmur a prayer before launching the canoe and jumping in at the last moment. Then, as now, he steered his craft with a paddle, peering out across the rumpled mass, seeking a lane of open water. As many as a dozen teams take part in the race, which is a high point of the annual Québec Carnaval today. Back in 1856, one man dared to face the ice simply because he wanted to meet his newly arrived fiancée.

Half in and half out of the twenty-eight-foot craft, alternately paddling, rowing, shoving, and hauling, an exhausted team faces the return journey across the river from Lévis to Québec. Because of the speed of the current, the round trip is actually triangular. In earlier days, before the terrifying trip became a race, the journey could take as long as six hours. Modern crews have made it in as little as forty-seven minutes. The five members of each team must be in superb condition. The Château Frontenac/Bodyguard team, which won the race for the sixth time in 1993, did endurance training throughout the year and worked out intensively on Nautilus equipment for six months. Eight weeks before the race, they worked on their stamina, climbing up the 400 steps from the river's edge to the Plains of Abraham. Rugged Canadians, indeed!

of ships in St. John's harbour, the *frost* that obscures our windows on February days, the *slush* we slop through during a Calgary chinook, the *hail* that hammers Saskatchewan barns, the *sleet* that slows traffic on Toronto's Gardiner Expressway, the *powder* that every skier in the Laurentians longs for, the *pack* that makes it possible to have snowball fights in Vancouver.

Winter is a scientific phenomenon under constant study, and scientists have sensibly adopted certain Inuit words, such as *quali* (snow that collects on trees). But there are other descriptions for falling frozen precipita-

Even before the line was completed, the Canadian Pacific Railway required monstrous snowploughs like this one to clear the line through the Rogers Pass. This photograph was made during the construction period in the 1880s.

tion—ten in all, according to the International Snow Classification System—ranging from *plates* and *stellars* to *spatial dendrites* and *graupel.* In 1966, two scientists, Magono and Lee, divided snow crystals into eighty categories, not including "miscellaneous."

Snow and ice have helped to dictate the shape and structure of Canada. The great glaciers that transformed the face of the land each began with a tiny patch of snow. The vast ice sheets, some two miles thick, had their birth when winter, in effect, became endless. That required a change in temperature of no more than a few degrees. As the sun's warmth diminished, the time came when some of one winter's snow remained to seed a growing snowfield the following season. As falling snow did not melt, the original patch grew imperceptibly, year after year, eon after eon. The snow piled up until its very weight compacted the crystals into ice. Creeping out in all directions like molasses poured from a jug in January, the ice reached as far south as St. Louis, Missouri. It advanced and retreated as many as twenty times, but we can trace with any accuracy only the final onslaught at the end of the Pleistocene Age.

Twenty thousand years ago, three vast Pleistocene ice sheets smothered much of the northern half of the continent. One, in the west, sprawled over the cordilleran spine; its remnants can be seen in the great glaciers of the southern Yukon and Alaska, in the Columbia Icefield on the Lake Louise-Jasper highway, and the Illecillewaet Glacier in the Selkirk Mountains.

In the centre, the Keewatin Ice Sheet, acting like a kind of bulldozer, scoured the overlying soil from the Precambrian Shield, destroying the drainage pattern of

A CPR snowplough struggles to clear a slide between the Rogers Pass and Glacier, B.C., in 1914. The boring of the longest double-track tunnel in the world—the five-mile-long Connaught—eliminated the line through the Rogers Pass.

the tundra but providing the prairies with the rich loam that helped create the Canadian wheat economy, and exposing the roots of ancient mountains to the prospector's pick. That ice sheet has retreated to the High Arctic, to Ellesmere Island and the ocean beyond; but its clawmarks can be seen today in the form of drumlin ridges between the slender lakes that radiate out from the centre, resembling, from the air, a ploughed field after a rainstorm. To the east, the remains of the Labrador Ice Sheet are found on the pocked surface of

On April 3, 1898, a terrifying slide on the Chilkoot Pass buried scores of Klondike stampeders under thirty feet of snow. Within thirty minutes more than a thousand men were at work with shovels trying to save the goldseekers from suffocation. At least sixty perished.

Northern Quebec and in the Barnes Ice Cap that straddles the peaks of Baffin Island. It is a mere ten thousand years since that ice retreated.

If glacial progress was imperceptible, the snow slides that thunder down the flanks of the Selkirks in midwinter race at such a speed that they create in front of them a windstorm known as a "flurry"—a tame enough name to give to a veritable cyclone that rips out everything in its path. The snowfall is phenomenal on the Selkirks' western slopes, for here the moist winds blowing in from the Pacific are blocked by the mountain rampart. On the summits, by midwinter, the snowfall can be deeper than sixty-five feet.

Heavy with water, the snowfields are easily dislodged from the slopes, creating an awesome spectacle. Picture over eight hundred thousand cubic feet of snow and ice roaring down the mountain flanks, seizing huge boulders and tossing them aside like marbles, ripping out great cedars, and compressing the air into the flurry that can snap off mature trees fifty feet above the base without uprooting them. One such cyclone was so powerful that it knocked eight loaded freight cars off the CPR tracks near Glacier, B.C. After one slide caused fifty-eight deaths, the railway company gave in to nature. It abandoned the original line through the Rogers Pass and bored a double-track tunnel—the longest in the world—through the bowels of Mount Macdonald to escape the perils of the rampaging snow.

Yet, in other manifestations, snow can be benign, and not only for outdoor sportsmen. As more than one traveller has discovered, it has insulating properties that make a snow cave a haven from the blasts of winter. In an older snowbank there are strata—just as there are in sedimentary rock—that provide science with a kind of chart depicting the season's laminated accumulation of snow. The space between the harder layers is used by small animals—mice, lemmings, voles—as runways and nesting sites. Plant stems, reaching up through the bank, provide vertical shafts that, with bubbles in the ice, supply oxygen to small vertebrates.

In snow and ice, then, there is life. In Frobisher Bay on Baffin Island, at least twenty animal species have been found in the ice, mostly nematode worms but also small shrimps and the larvae of worms and shellfish. These live on microscopic algae of which no fewer than 227 species have been found, alive and functioning, embedded in ice.

In my Yukon youth a favourite practical joke was to hoax newcomers by serving them an "ice worm cocktail," using small pieces of spaghetti coiled into a martini. Some of these *cheechakos* actually believed that worms lived in the ice, and we chuckled over their naïveté as they gagged on the drink. Now I discover that they were right. Science has given them the last laugh.

FROZEN CRYSTALS

Water in its solid state takes many forms, as the photographs on the following pages show. These exquisite images demonstrate that there is as much variety in snow, frost, and ice as there is in sand and sparkling sea—a truth known to all Canadians but not so apparent to those who view our environment from afar.

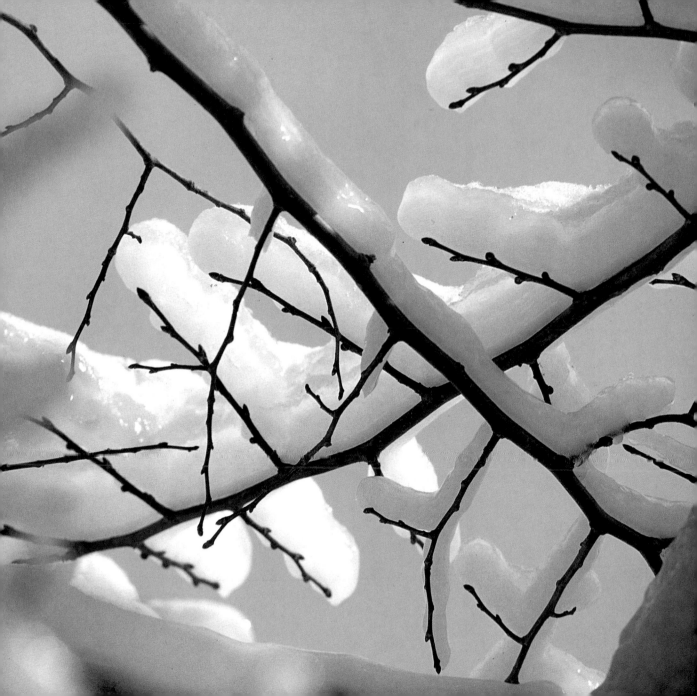

OLD TYME WINTER

OLD TYME WINTER: THE IMAGES THAT THAT PHRASE evokes are almost invariably nostalgic—appealing, even comforting, and, yes, *warm.* What a word to apply to the memory of a climate so frigid it could freeze the eyelids together! But we were all children once, and the memories of childhood and winter are intertwined. We cannot divorce ourselves from our cultural clichés: *sleigh-bells ringing, children singing. . . chestnuts roasting by an open fire. . . dashing through the snow, in a one-horse open sleigh. . . over the river to grandmother's house . . .walking in a winter wonderland.* We are the play-things of Tin Pan Alley, the targets of the greeting-card companies, the clients of the calendar artists, and, to be candid, fervent worshippers at the shrines of our own schools of landscape art, some of which are represented in this book.

They have all presided over the prettification of winter. Who has not been willingly seduced by the Krieghoffs and the Gagnons, with their portrayals of merry-making habitants disporting themselves before snow-covered taverns, or laughing families pulled on ornate sleighs behind scampering horses? Who has not been charmed by A.Y. Jackson's sinuous, snow-covered roads, or Lawren Harris's snow-blown evergreens?

Yet there was a time in early Canada when winter was a horror to those who faced its blasts and other, later times when men and women froze to death, unable to reach civilization's warmth.

My own childhood was haunted by such tales. Fresh in our minds was the tragedy of the Lost Patrol in the Wind River country to the north. The bodies of four Mounted Policemen were found by a colleague, Corporal W.J.D. Dempster, whose name has since been enshrined on the highway that now winds through those windswept wastes. Dempster found two of the corpses stiff beside a dead fire. A six-inch tree, hacked down by a blunt axe in an attempt to keep the embers alive, lay a few feet away.

My mother used to tell of a trapper, frozen to death at his door as he struggled to enter his cabin, not far from Whitehorse. His body was frozen into the shape of a cross, arms outstretched, legs spread-eagled. The undertaker, who came in from Skagway, was forced to wait several days before the corpse could be thawed into shape for the coffin.

In the cities winter can be hell. "Bag ladies," as the

This is the image of old tyme winter that remains with us: horse-drawn sleighs cantering gently along the snow-covered streets. That was fine for the well-to-do, but for ordinary citizens, winter was not so idyllic. This is Sherbrooke Street, Montreal, in 1885.

press calls them, make headlines only when their bodies are discovered frozen in an abandoned truck (the fate of Diane Joubert, aged forty-one, in 1985) or in the stairwell of an apartment building (Eugenia Balcombe, sixty-six, in 1991). But most winter deaths these days are the result of heart attacks suffered by those who try to shovel the snow from their own sidewalks. Others die in traffic accidents blamed on the weather. In 1989, a single storm caused the deaths of thirteen people in British Columbia.

For the early fur traders the winter was dismal, uncomfortable, and sometimes disastrous. The explorer David Thompson called it "Siberian" and declared that the Lord had, mercifully, fitted the Indian "to live and enjoy his cold region of forest and deserts of snow." The white man, Thompson said, was unequal to such a climate.

In those days the winter season was defined by two dates: those of the autumn freeze-up and the spring break-up. Once the lakes and rivers froze, the early Canadians faced up to seven months of immobility. In the late eighteenth century, Duncan Cameron, a fur trader, wrote wanly of the chill land north of Lake Superior. "The winters are very long and severe. Some years it may be reckoned from the 15th of October to the latter end of May." Small wonder, then, that the motto of the Montreal Beaver Club, the exclusive society of wintering partners of the North West Company, was "Fortitude in Distress." No one could be a member unless he had endured at least one winter in the Northwest.

On the English River north of Lake Superior in the winter of 1792-93, William MacKay, a North West Company trader, stayed alive only by eating a concoc-

tion of boiled lichens. "I rely believe," he wrote, in his fractured spelling, "that no man that ever Came to this Country had so much hardship in so short a time." That same season, a fellow fur trader, Alexander Mackenzie, wrote to his nephew, "I begin to think this is the height of folly in a man to reside in a country of this kind deprived of every comfort that can render life agreeable." Two years later Duncan McGillivray wrote to his uncle, Simon McTavish, complaining about the "dull and gloomy prospects" before him and the "many uncomfortable years" he would be forced to pass "in ignorance and solitude."

In the winter of 1810-11, four men wintering in the Mackenzie River district were reduced to living for three months on dried beaver skins. Three died. The survivor, Ferdinand Wentzel, a man who had endured twelve winters in the Northwest, described that year as "the most melancholy and most disastrous that could ever have befallen to any one single man to support without becoming torpidly stupid or totally senseless."

As David D. Kemp has pointed out in a recent study, the hardships of the old time Canadian winter were mental as well as physical. When David Thompson made his epic trip through the Athabasca Pass to the Columbia River in the winter of 1810-11, four of his men deserted and returned east. Kemp points out that "mental distress was largely responsible for the defection."

The Scots traders were a rugged breed, used to physical toil. They had to be, as Robert Campbell's epic trip in the winter of 1852-53 demonstrates. When the Chilkat Indians destroyed the Hudson's Bay Company's fort at the confluence of the Pelly and Yukon rivers,

Canadians loved to have their portraits taken showing them muffled to the ears, defying a studio blizzard made by spraying Japan white on the photographic plate. Tourist promoters, like the CPR's William Van Horne, were not amused.

convivial Frobisher sought out company at the Beaver Club or the local officers' mess.

Lesser mortals also enjoyed the long winter lull. "We had six months' holiday in trade," wrote young Thomas Storrow Brown of those days. "There were no railroads or telegraphs to keep merchants and their clerks under whip to spur them all the time. Merchants waited for spring to work. On the other hand, all would devote themselves to frolic and jollity. . . . Winter is an ideal season for carousing."

"At some dinners," Brown recalled, "all were expected to get drunk, and lest any should be delinquent, the door would be locked to keep them from escaping." Brown, who came to Canada in 1818, recalled in 1870 that few of his old cronies had survived such drinking bouts. "Merchants and clerks indulged so freely that I . . . remember less than six of all the young men and lads I then knew, who have survived the consequences. Theirs was a short and merry life, ending too often before the age of thirty. . . ."

For the young men about town, then, the winter was, in Collard's phrase, "a season of hectic idleness." But for those who were thrown out of work it was the cruellest of seasons, as it can be today. The poor froze and starved, for there were no social services to aid them. As jobs decreased, wages dropped, following the laws of supply and demand. Contemporary accounts from the periodicals of those times reveal little of this side of winter. As the *Dominion Illustrated* commented in January 1891, "with snow and frost comes brightness

and cheer, good spirits and invigorating amusements." The poor had neither the time nor the ability to write of their misery. They would not have agreed with the anonymous editorial writer that "our cold winters, instead of being a drawback . . . are in reality a substantial boon and mean a thriving business for our merchants, vigour in body and mind for our citizens, and pleasure for all healthy lads and lasses."

It is the rural areas of the nineteenth century that have provided us with our traditional image of the Old Tyme Winter. In the countryside, where food was grown and stored for winter use, the dark days constituted a lively social season complete with balls, dance parties, sleighing excursions, and, of course, courtship and marriage. It was this image that an article in *The Beaver* evoked in 1991 when the magazine waxed enthusiastic about the "old optimistic Canada" when our ancestors "stepped out into the winter weather with bounding enthusiasm," spending "hours in the open air on frozen ponds and ice-bound rivers, walking in the winter woods or skimming along country roads in sleighs drawn by puffing horses." I live today in the countryside, and those phrases describe identical weekend pleasures in the out-of-doors; the only difference is that the sleighs have been replaced by snowmobiles. In the cities, where most of the population now lives, such pursuits are not as easily available.

"Canada, for all its frost and snow, was a good place to live," *The Beaver* commented. But not for the poor in the tenements of Montreal, Quebec, and Toronto,

A century ago, a winter fire could be a horror. The water from the hose truck froze solid as soon as it hit the building, encasing it in a ragged garment of ice—that is, if the hose itself didn't crack open in the cold.

condemned to harsh exposure in an age that did not welcome public charity. To them these nostalgic sentiments would seem hollow indeed.

Some writers recall with awe the big snows of the past, suggesting that winters were fiercer a century or so ago than they are today. Canada does seem to have been warming up since the turn of the century. In Toronto, the mean annual temperature has increased from 7.7 degrees Celsius to 9.1, in Montreal from 5.2 to 7.4, in Fredericton from 4.7 to 5.3, in Regina from 1 degree to 3.4. Much of this, however, is illusory. As the cities grow, as more buildings sprout up, as more people crowd in, the temperature rises. Toronto, for instance, is, on the average, two degrees warmer than it would have been had no city existed on the site today.

Photographs taken in the nineteenth century show mountains of snow clogging the city streets. But we forget that in those days there was no such thing as civic snow clearance. In Montreal, every citizen was required by law to shovel the space in front of his house as soon as the storm ended or by nine o'clock in the morning. Similar laws exist today, but now the accumulation is speedily removed—melted by a salt solution that causes automobiles to rust, or carted off through the use of trucks and ploughs. In the early days, the snow was allowed to pile higher and higher in the roadway until a man going for a stroll down his street could not see his neighbour on the opposite side. Soon the mountains of snow towered above the Victorian houses, and it is these photographs that call up the idea of a harsher, more demanding winter than the one we know today.

Official snow clearance did not begin until this century. (In Montreal, for instance, the civic authorities resisted tax-supported snow removal until 1905.) And thus, for decades, as the photographs on these pages show, pedestrians in Canadian cities seem to have been trudging through Alpine mountain passes. A stroll to the corner shop became an adventure—a bracing hike, a challenge. The Anglican Bishop of Montreal, Ashton Oxenden, a transplanted Englishman, regarded himself as "the most persevering pedestrian in the place." But this lover of exercise and fresh air found he had to don an early version of a mountaineer's crampon in order to make his way in safety down the slippery, snowy streets and avenues of his adopted city.

THE ARTIST'S WINTER

By and large, the painters who tempted the winter cold in Canada left a legacy of comfortable art. Winter was depicted as benign—a time for sliding and sleighing and for soft snowflakes drifting down from the skies. The shrieking winds, the raging blizzards, and the eerie whiteouts have rarely been depicted in watercolours and oils, probably because the artists themselves stayed resolutely indoors, to venture outside only when the skies cleared and the temperature rose to the point where the pigments no longer froze on their palettes.

Robert Todd *The Ice Cone, Montmorency Falls* c.1850
oil on canvas 34.2 x 45.9 cm
National Gallery of Canada

J.E.H. MacDonald *Tracks and Traffic* 1912
oil on canvas 71.1 x 106.6 cm
Art Gallery of Ontario

Tom Thomson *Wood Interior, Winter* (detail) c.1915
oil on panel 21.9 x 26.7 cm
McMichael Canadian Art Collection

Albert H. Robinson *A Church in Westmount* 1923
oil on canvas 22" x 26"
National Gallery of Canada

Paul Kane *Winter Travelling* (detail) 1848
oil on canvas 21" x 29"
Royal Ontario Museum

L. L. FitzGerald *Williamson's Garage* 1927
oil on canvas 55.9 x 45.7 cm
National Gallery of Canada

A.Y. Jackson *First Snow, Algoma* (detail) c.1919-20
oil on canvas 107.71 x 127.7 cm
McMichael Canadian Art Collection

THE BIG
STORMS

I**T IS A VERY CANADIAN PHENOMENON. OTHER COUN-**tries regularly await hurricanes and typhoons, tornadoes, waterspouts, or tidal waves. In Canada from November to March, we have blizzards. No section of the country is immune, from balmy Victoria, which dug itself out of a four-foot snowfall on Boxing Day in 1968, to Heart's Content, Newfoundland, where on January 5, 1963, even the snowploughs were driven off the roads. We have learned to brace ourselves for blizzards. The details are familiar: highways turned into parking lots, cars abandoned, power cut off, deliveries impossible, schools closed, travel at an impasse—men and women dead from heart attacks, exposure, or traffic accidents. We pay a high price, in this mechanized age, for the fury of winter.

Everybody remembers the Big Storm of the past—the blizzard that broke all records, the blizzard that was "the worst in living memory," the one that we each use as a defining moment in our lives. "That was the year of the Big Storm," people say. In Regina they remember the Big Storm of January 30, 1947—the worst in Canadian railway history. In Montreal they remember the Big Storm of March 4, 1971, when the city endured the greatest single day's snowfall on record. In Saint John they remember the Big Storm of February 16, 1959, when fifteen-foot drifts blocked the streets and brought the community to a standstill. On Prince Edward Island they remember the Big Storm of February 22, 1982, that marooned everybody for five days. In Iqaluit on Baffin Island, they remember the Big Storm of February 8, 1979, which kept the residents imprisoned indoors for ten days. In Vancouver some still recall the Big Storm of January 19, 1943, when streetcars rose up on the ice-packed tracks and slithered off the rails. And in Victoria some still talk about the Big Storm of February 4, 1916, when the streets of that verdant city were waist-deep in snow—an unexpected disaster that the city's single snowplough could not handle.

The Big Storm that I remember was the record blizzard that hit southern Ontario and Quebec, from Windsor to Quebec City, on December 13, 1944. I remember it because I was trying to get home to Vancouver for Christmas from the Royal Military College in Kingston. Toronto was at the centre of the storm, and our train, already hours late, was forced to wait for more long hours outside a city that had been rendered helpless by a fall of more than twenty-two inches of snow. Buses were immo-

The photograph opposite and those on the following pages speak for themselves. The setting is Saint John, N.B., December 30, 1993; but most of these pictures could have been taken almost anywhere in Canada that winter. Here, as revellers prepared to welcome in the New Year, some seven inches of snow had already fallen, traffic was almost non-existent, shopping malls were forced to close, and airline flights were cancelled. Not a major storm, just a typical one.

bilized. Taxis could not operate. All traffic, except for emergency vehicles, had been banned from the clogged streets. Anybody who wanted to try to get to work—and there was an astonishing number of these—was forced to trudge for blocks through heavy drifts. Only people who happened to have skis had an easy trip, like Arthur Irwin, the editor of *Maclean's*, who slalomed all the way from North Toronto to the corner of University and Dundas, or Bette Hodgins, who worked for the weather bureau on Bloor Street and was determined to propel herself to the front door.

As is so often the case, the city's equipment was inadequate to handle an unexpected disaster. Plants making war materiel were closed. Funerals were postponed. Expectant mothers walked to the hospitals, where all but major surgery was cancelled. There was no milk delivery, no bread. Mothers with small children trudged to the local firehall where such necessities were available on short ration. The telephone switchboards were so jammed with long-distance inquiries that two hundred women operators were issued with toothbrushes and nightgowns by the army and put up at a makeshift dormitory. The city stood still. Eaton's and Simpsons closed. For the first time in its long history, the venerable *Globe and Mail* was unable to publish. The mayor organized a phalanx of "storm commandos" (this was, after all, the height of the Second World War) and detailed fourteen hundred to help clear the streets. Two hundred trucks were needed to haul the snow away. Finally, with a lurch and a rattle, our train puffed into Union Station, a day late, and in the end we made it home to the West Coast for the Yule season.

There have been worse storms recorded, going all

the way back to the one in Ottawa in April 1885, when a vicious blizzard dropped a total of forty-two inches of snow on the capital in what old-timers called the longest continuous storm in memory. The snow fell without pause for fifty-two hours, causing the roof of the Royal Museum Theatre, next door to the Central Station, to collapse under its weight with a loud crash. Local residents thought a powder magazine had exploded, especially as the resultant rubble caused a pillar of dust, like smoke, to rise from the ruins. Fortunately there were no deaths; the theatre was empty because the blizzard had forced cancellation of the matinee. Almost a century later, on February 28, 1984, Ottawa was brought to a standstill by another blizzard, so fierce that snowploughs couldn't handle it. Pedestrians shunned the streets, but one man, apparently, revelled in the storm. Pierre Elliott Trudeau took a long walk in the snow that night, feeling "very combative," listened to his heart, and decided to quit politics.

On March 4, 1971, Montrealers awoke to discover that the already deep snowdrifts had climbed as far as the second storey of their homes and, on occasion, beyond the eaves. This was the greatest single day's fall of snow on record. Over the course of the storm, electricity was cut off for as long as a week. The mayor himself cancelled the hockey game between the Vancouver Canucks and the Montreal Canadiens because he feared a panic if the power failed at the Forum. It was the only time in NHL history that a hockey game was put off because of the weather. None of the three morning papers was able to publish, but, as in so many similar urban storms throughout Canada, there was surprisingly little crime. It was just as difficult for thieves to get around as for honest citizens. One drugstore, however, was robbed of sixty-five dollars at the height of the storm. The miscreants escaped on a snowmobile.

The word "blizzard" is often used by the press to identify any winter storm that causes inconvenience. But the weather experts define it more specifically. A real blizzard is a violent winter storm combining freezing temperatures and a very strong wind, at least twenty-five miles in velocity an hour and so laden with falling or blowing snow that visibility is reduced to half a mile for at least three hours.

When the weather turns ugly, modern mechanization takes a back seat. Drivers on the great postwar superhighways are helpless when storms strike; so are the diesel locomotives. In January 1947, near Regina, in a blizzard that raged for ten days, an entire CPR train was buried in a gigantic snowdrift over half a mile long and twenty-six feet deep. In Ottawa that March, when twenty-five inches of snow paralyzed the city, sleighs came out of mothballs to replace trucks, until the horses themselves were so exhausted that milk deliveries ceased. Expectant mothers were conveyed to hospitals on toboggans. Fire trucks could not reach burning buildings, let alone an overheated car that burst into flames. Spectators on the scene improvised with handfuls of snow to douse the blaze.

On a fifteen-mile stretch of Highway 401 east of London, Ontario, on November 24, 1970, the winds were so fierce and the snow so heavy that the traffic took six hours to move one mile. Some drivers were trapped in their cars for fourteen hours, huddled together in

light clothing, numbed by the cold, and so hungry that they pleaded with other stranded motorists for food. Seven hundred vehicles were mired axle-deep in the snow that day.

This section of Southern Ontario is a snow belt, prone to blizzards. In late January 1971, on Highway 401, hundreds of gallons of milk had to be dumped because trucks could not get through a litter of abandoned vehicles. And when one trailer carrying eight thousand gallons of raw whiskey overturned, police had to be called to guard it. Service centres were so crowded children slept on storeroom shelves. The former premier, John Robarts, stranded for twenty-five hours on the highway, was taunted by hecklers who threw his party's slogan back at him: "Is there any place you'd rather be?" During the Big Storm of December 1977, one London citizen who had abandoned his car mushed through the snow to a telephone booth to let his wife know he was all right and would soon be home. While he was speaking, a snowplough passed, trapping him in the booth. That month the depth of snow in the city reached twenty-eight inches.

In the superstorm of 1978 near Woodstock, three members of a Toronto family died of asphyxiation in their snowbound car. But when snowmobilers arrived on the scene, they found a tiny, four-year-old girl alive in the back seat. The same morning, Barbara Edwards of St. Thomas left her home accompanied by her nine-month-old baby, little knowing that she would spend twelve hours trapped in her car before the whiteout lifted slightly and she could see well enough to walk the five hundred yards to the nearest farmhouse. Another

Notman's first composite photograph, of a skating carnival in Montreal's Victoria Rink during the winter of 1870, hangs in the McCord Museum. It looks like an oil painting thanks to the work of Henry Sandham, who helped to revolutionize the technique of painting over photographs. The cream of Montreal society is shown here, not to mention Prince Arthur himself (in a fur hat at the top left) and the wife of Colonel Garnet Wolseley, the Red River uprising campaigner who would become commander-in-chief of the British Army (she's to the right of the Prince). The young girl whose studio portrait is shown above, unretouched, skates at the extreme right, fitting neatly into the throng.

Notman's skill created the speeding toboggan at right from the static photo at left.

Prominent Montrealers of both sexes, many of whom are easily identifiable in the finished work, traipsed to Notman's studio, bringing their elegant costumes. There, in a special dressing room, they were outfitted and coiffured by Notman's staff before being clamped in a variety of attitudes in the new posing stands and photographed in natural light.

When the final work was assembled and rephotographed, it was transferred to a canvas washed with a solution of potassium cyanide and caustic potash. It was then iodized with a solution of egg whites, honey, potassium iodide, and water. Finally it was sensitized with a compound of silver nitrate, acetic acid, and potassium iodide. The negative was immediately exposed on the still-wet canvas (requiring a longer exposure time than light-sensitive paper) and fixed. At that point the painters—Henry Sandham and Edward Sharpe—went to work to colour the result.

Notman died in 1891. Two of his sons took over the business. By the mid-1930s, when the 35mm "candid camera" made its appearance, the Notman style of winter photography was no longer popular and certainly no longer necessary. In 1935, Associated Screen News acquired the Notman firm and with it half a million Notman negatives. By then, only a few historians were aware of the Notman record. The negatives remained boxed in the ASN basement for twenty years, half-forgotten and gathering dust.

In 1956, one hundred years almost to the day after William Notman arrived in Montreal, the newsreel company decided to dispense with the collection. If nobody wanted it, the priceless trove of negatives would be destroyed. Few realized at that time just how precious they were, but *Maclean's* magazine was interested. I was then managing editor and was sent to Montreal to see if the pictures were worth saving and publishing.

I had not then heard of William Notman and knew nothing of his work, and so the photographs, all meticulously filed, were a revelation. After a week, in which I looked over all of the Notman prints from 1856 to 1891, I reported that we had uncovered an invaluable photographic record of nineteenth-century Canada that should certainly be preserved. *Maclean's* then bought the collection for $10,000 and, after it had used the photographs for a series of picture stories, donated it to the McCord Museum in Montreal, where it now rests—the only monument that William Notman would ever have wanted or needed.

THE EVOLUTION
OF WINTER PLAY

WHAT HAS BECOME OF THE GREAT WINTER SPORTS of the past? The snowshoers in their blanket coats and tuques, the iceboaters skimming over the smooth surfaces of a dozen freshwater bays, the tobogganers racing down the steep man-made slopes—all these belong to a time when indoor electronic amusements did not exist and people thought nothing of venturing into the cold to make their own fun.

The great fad of the 1880s was tobogganing. "Everybody has gone crazy on the subject, and men, women, and children revel in the dashing flight," a Canadian enthusiast reported to New York's *Century* magazine in 1885. The huge cone at Montmorency Falls provided a natural toboggan slide for Quebeckers. Others built special runs—dizzy wooden inclines suspended from high towers. A spirit of revelry abounded. "The hills are lit by torches stuck in the snow on each side of the track, and huge bonfires are kept burning, around which gather picturesque groups." In Europe, tobogganing fathered the faster sport of bobsledding, but not in Canada. When the first Canadian bobsled team travelled to the Olympics, there wasn't a bobsled run in all of Canada. And by

that time, tobogganing was confined largely to children.

There was a time when Toronto Harbour was alive with as many as fifty iceboats skimming at unbelievable speeds under great triangular sails between the shore and Toronto Island. By the early 1890s, their occupants were able to travel faster than any other human beings in the world. In 1907, it was claimed, one iceboat actually reached the astonishing speed of 152 miles per hour. Certainly in 1911, when a famous iceboat named *Comet* competed with a motorcycle, the two finished in a dead heat. But where are the iceboaters today? By the 1930s they had gone the way of the tobogganers. The presence of ice-breaking tugs helped to speed their demise.

And yet the oldest winter sport of all—curling—has survived and prospered. Why? Surely because it was the most democratic. You didn't have to be a member of the upper crust to curl. In the early days all you needed were some "rocks" made of kettles filled with sand and a set of ordinary kitchen brooms. The nearest small pond acted as a rink. The game goes back to Scotland and was first introduced into Canada, so it is said, in the 1770s by Scottish troops on garrison duty. Officially it

Prince Arthur obviously loved winter sports. Here he is with a group of friends, tobogganing at Rideau Hall in the winter of 1870.

began in Montreal in 1807, when the first curling club was organized by twenty Scotsmen playing with cast-iron stones, a development that apparently caused a culture shock among the habitants. One French-speaking farmer's reaction was recorded in the minute book of the newly formed club: "Today I saw a band of Scots, who were throwing large balls of iron, made like kettles, on the ice, after which they shouted, 'Soup, Soup!' Then they laughed like madmen. I do believe they are mad."

Thanks largely to the Scots, the pastime quickly spread, first to Quebec City and Halifax, then to Upper Canada. John Galt's Canada Company attracted Scottish immigrants, and by the mid-1830s, from Kingston to Guelph curling clubs were formed, the members using "stones" cut from the trunks of birch or maple trees and bound with iron bands to prevent the wood from splitting. The game has never lost its Scottish flavour. In my father's day in the Yukon, first prize was always a case of Johnnie Walker Black Label.

When the Pacific railway was built in the 1880s, curling moved west. The long, dry prairie winters were ideal for the outdoor game before the now familiar covered rinks were built—rinks that served as community centres in little towns all along the route of the CPR. When the floor was flooded, the resultant ice sheet could last as long as four months. "Nowhere in the world is there such a depth of curling skill as in Canada," David B. Smith, a historian of the sport, has written. The Selkirk settlers at Red River, all Scottish immigrants, curled long before the railway arrived.

In 1915, the heyday of iceboat racing, this was a familiar spectacle on the frozen surface of Toronto Harbour. In the background: Toronto Island.

Today, Manitoba is the centre of the curling world. Western rinks dominate the international bonspiels, and the game now attracts one million Canadian men and women.

Curling outlasted tobogganing and the other nineteenth-century social pastimes because, with its Scottish roots and its small-town western background, it was a sport for the people. That could not be said of snowshoeing or "tramping," as it was called. Snowshoeing was more than a sport: to the upper classes, it was a social designation. Snowshoe organizations, which took their cue from the daddy of them all, the Montreal Snow Shoe Club, were snobbish and highly exclusive. How bitterly ironic! The Indians, who invented the snowshoe, couldn't belong.

The tuque, the familiar blanket coat and sash, once the accustomed winter wear of the coureur de bois, became symbols of social class. No native Canadian could wear the club's official uniform, and no woman, either. Through the device of the blackball, social snowshoeing was reserved for white, male, Anglo-Saxon Protestants—those who could afford to take a carriage down to Mr. Notman's portrait studio to have themselves photographed in a variety of manly winter poses.

"Manly" was the operative word. The snowshoeing craze fitted easily into an era that equated moral rectitude and religious fervour with athletic prowess. Some groups, such as the St. George Snowshoeing Club, whose members were known as Saints, saw themselves as modern heirs of the knights of old. George Beers,

snowshoeing's greatest promoter, wrote ecstatically in an American magazine of "hundreds of muscular Christians yclept Saints of St. George, running wild in blanket coat and tuque over Mount Royal. . . intent on no better mission than the development of their muscles."

Beers was the most enthusiastic of those nationalists who equated the invigorating climate and manly sports with what they insisted was a superior Canadian character. "Of all the winter characteristics in Canada," Beers wrote in the *Century*, "snowshoeing reigns supreme. It is the true, natural revel of robust 'Canucks' who love the snow, however deep, and the storm, however stiff."

Snowshoeing was not just manly and invigorating; it also required "fortitude, courage, and perseverance." The clean, crisp air, it was claimed, had had a moral effect on outdoor Canadians. By keeping out "the weaker races" it had produced "a hardy race of the north."

This boastful elitism, which we would today call racism, was extended to membership in the snowshoe clubs. Old men and boys were allowed to race, but women, so the sexist snowshoers declared, could only aspire to marry a snowshoe man. By the 1860s, when the sport was developing along two lines, the original "tramping" and the competitive racing and steeplechasing, women weren't even allowed to tramp. The best they could do was to *stroll*.

From its adoption by Europeans snowshoeing had been as much a social undertaking as a sport. In the

Curling was a winter sport as much for women as for men—in spite of the voluminous clothing. This is a women's curling team in pre-Great War Winnipeg.

Nonetheless, for years skiing remained an obscure sport. No one in Canada manufactured skis; few if any retail stores carried them. There was no skiing technique: the first skiers simply pointed themselves downhill and shoved off. They had only one pole, sometimes none. The only ski wax came from tallow candles. As for skiing costumes, the skiers wore anything available. At the turn of the century they careered down the slopes swathed in heavy clothing, looking like stuffed animals. Light nylon skiwear has been a boon to the sport.

Skiing prospered because it moved with the times. In the old days, thrill seekers challenged the slopes with ordinary overshoes strapped to primitive skis. In skating, striking advances in both shoe and skate design between 1830 and 1860 had made sophisticated figure skating possible, so that by 1890 a Canadian, Louis Rubenstein, became the unofficial champion amateur figure skater of the world. Skiing followed suit with advances of its own, including development of new footwear that clicked easily onto modern skis.

What we have been seeing, really, is the mechanization of winter play. The snowmobile has replaced the toboggan. The ski-tow has taken the sweat out of the uphill side of the downhill runs. Ski trains to the Laurentians, modern highways to such remote places as British Columbia's Whistler resort have put the slopes within reach of everybody. Even the highest peaks in the Rockies can now be reached by helicopter. Curling, figure skating, skiing, and, of course, ice hockey, have become spectator sports, thanks to television. Only cross-country skiing, the newest national fad, demands the kind of energy that the old-time activities required. That is the legacy of the remarkable Jackrabbit Johannsen, whose influence cannot be underestimated.

It is salutary to note that Jackrabbit took up cross-country skiing at the age of 2½ and kept at it for all of his remarkably long life. When he died in 1986 he was 111½ years old. Couch potatoes take note.

A winter trotting race with sleighs in Newfoundland: a forgotten sport, date unknown.

SNOW PLAY

The great Canadian outdoor sports—hockey, figure skating, curling—have either gone professional or moved indoors, leaving the ponds and the snow-covered slopes largely to amateurs. But you can't ski indoors, nor can the newest of the winter sports, snowmobiling, be confined within four walls. The youthful medal winners of the future must still learn their craft out of doors, where winter sport is mostly for fun, even when the stiff breezes blow.

Above: *Entire families, dressed in the colours of winter, slide down the steep slopes of the Plains of Abraham where Wolfe and Montcalm once did battle.*

Right: *Like bright insects buzzing across the alabaster flanks of the Rockies, the Banff Ski Patrol keeps a wary eye out for those in trouble.*

Winter play in the shadow of two venerable Canadian landmarks...

Above: *Young Quebeckers roll in the snow at the Château Frontenac.*

Right: *The longest skating rink in the world—the frozen Rideau River—begins at the Château Laurier and seems to go on forever.*

Overleaf: *The great Canadian sport of ice fishing (here at Lac St-Pierre, Quebec) demands a portable hut and infinite patience.*

Above: *At Cole Harbour, N.S., a father helps tie his son's snowshoes.*
They look very much like the ones my father once strapped on me.

Left: *My grandson, Orin, and his friend, Brandy, make angels in the snow,*
just as my sister and I did nearly seventy years ago.

Above: *The modern snowmobile, a Canadian invention, has not only changed winter sport but has also affected winter fashion.*

Right: *In spite of the mechanization of winter sport, cross-crountry skiing has become a popular fad. In Quebec City, enthusiasts don't have to go far to reach le Parc-des-Champs-de Bataille.*

Above: *At Verret, N.B., on a December afternoon, a family puts the final touches on two snowmen, complete with woollen scarves.*

Left: *When I was a boy, nobody in our community owned skis. But in the last half century, skiing has become a craze as well as a sport.*

The snowmobile craze has given birth to a new professional sport, complete with formula machines, like the one at left, shown in action at St-Gabriel-de-Brandon in December 1993. This is one winter sport that Canadians can claim without dispute; the snowmobile was invented and developed by the Bombardier company not far from here. Snowmobile racing has all the thrills of the Indy circuit—and more. With engines roaring, drivers snap their clutches as soon as the starting flag drops, revving their engines to 6,000 rpm to achieve speeds of 100 mph. There's so much noise involved as the machines roar around the circuit that knowing fans wear ear protection. Snowmobiling has come a long way since the first Ski-Doo.

MAKING THE BEST OF WINTER

WINTER IS THE ONE SEASON THAT SEEMS INTER-minable. Although we greet the first feathery fall of snow with pleasure, we are fed up with it by February. "*Will it never end?*" we ask, knowing that the bitter winds of March still lie ahead. Only a minority can escape to the subtropical seas; the rest of us must put up with what we have. And so we make the best of winter, indulging in games and frivolity, in contests and "snowfests" designed to prove that winter can be *fun*.

And so it can be—at least for a week or a ten-day stretch of dancing, drinking, gambolling, and pumped-up merriment, specifically created to banish the February "blahs." Almost every community in Canada today has found a way of celebrating winter. These range from Prince George's Mardi Gras Snow Daze in British Columbia, through Ottawa's Winter-lude on the world's largest skating rink, to the Happy Valley–Goose Bay winter carnival in Labrador, set in Canada's most snowed-on community (160 inches a year). February has become the month for dog der-bies, snowmobile jamborees, ice sculptures, toboggan slides, skating contests, and in Quebec the ritual guz-zling of *caribou*, the potent tipple of *whiskey blanc*

and port sold in the basements of private homes dur-ing carnival week.

There must be more than two hundred winter festivals every February across Canada. Most are called *carnivals*, a word with Italian roots that suggests the traditional period of merrymaking immediately preceding the self-denial of Lent.

The idea was launched by the Montreal Snow Shoe Club at a time when the manly art was losing support, and the carnival served briefly to mask snowshoeing's decline. In 1882, Robert Davidson McGibbon, a twenty-four-year-old lawyer who was the club's vice-president, replying to a toast to "Our Winter Sports," asked, "Why not call in the world to see us in all the gaiety and fervour of our winter sports?" The response was enthusiastic and the results satisfying. As the Montreal *Gazette* exclaimed: "We hear no more of the terror of our Canadian winter. It is the Winter Carnival now that strangers talk and write about."

The centrepiece at that carnival and others that followed in Quebec City, Ottawa, and St. Paul, Min-nesota, was the gigantic palace constructed of huge blocks of ice (in this case cut from the St. Lawrence and erected in Dominion Square). This palace and

This imposing palace, more than a hundred feet tall, was built entirely of blocks of ice cut from the St. Lawrence River for the Montreal carnival of 1885.

Above: Carnaval *is a Christian celebration—a last frenzy of frivolity before the self-denial of Lent. That doesn't inhibit one enthusiast from carving a huge snow sculpture of the Buddha.*

Left: *It isn't Christmas; it's a look forward to Easter, here on the streets of Rue Sous-le-Fort.*

The master of the carnival, Bonhomme Carnaval, *Canada's most famous snowman, holds court during the parades that brighten the carnival nights. Wearing a sixty-pound fibreglass suit,* Bonhomme, *whose identity is kept a secret, continually urges the crowd to laugh and make merry.*

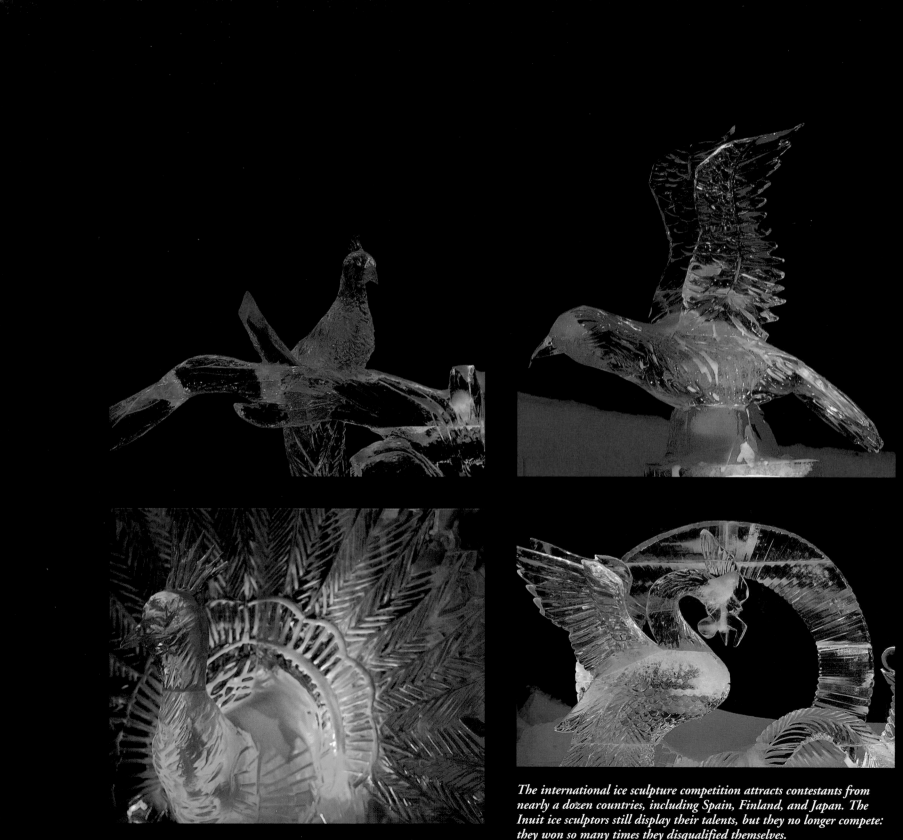

The international ice sculpture competition attracts contestants from nearly a dozen countries, including Spain, Finland, and Japan. The Inuit ice sculptors still display their talents, but they no longer compete: they won so many times they disqualified themselves.

Above: *Amateur artists abound at* Carnaval, *especially among the residents of the Rue Ste-Thérèse in Lower Town, where imaginative carvings turn the open spaces into a sculpture gallery, the subjects ranging from reproductions of the* Titanic *to Mickey Mouse himself.*

Left: *The tradition of the ice palace continues at the Quebec carnival, often attracting foreign television crews, as this one did in 1993. More than eighty feet high, it was the centrepiece of the festivities. Here the eternally smiling* Bonhomme *offered the crown to the carnival queen.*

Thousands of Canadian parents find themselves playing the national game vicariously as they watch over their offspring, hoping, perhaps, to nurture a future Gretzky or simply to make sure the kids are having fun and staying free of injury.

Pond Inlet is a community of youngsters. Half the population—five hundred in all—is under the age of twenty. There's a flourishing high school, but on days like this, with winter coming to an end and the spring sun rising from the frozen sea, schoolchildren are given a holiday to gambol in the snow on the mountainous icebergs.

The Peterloosie family of Pond Inlet has made a determined effort to keep alive the art of drum dancing and the singing of "ayaya" songs. They are, in fact, the only family group that performs in public for special events, although a local theatre company also puts on drum dances as part of its productions. Very few elders who can pick up a drum and dance and sing are left, and they do not do so on a regular basis. At Tqakijualuk High School an attempt has been made to encourage students to take an interest in the "ayaya" songs, which are most often accompanied by the drum. The singing of such songs began to die out after the missionaries arrived in 1929 and tried to wipe out what they felt was a pagan heritage. Now dancing and drumming are starting to come back. The Peterloosies have trained their teenaged son, Michael, to help revive a cultural tradition.

Jacob Attakaarlik Peterloosie is shown above and at right. With him is Annie Paingut Peterloosie and little Tommy.

The weather was so good on the day this photograph was made that school was cancelled and the students poured out on the sea ice for dog races and games.

The appearance of caribou herds on their regular migrations, shown at right on Utuk Lake near Pond Inlet, is another reason for rejoicing. Traditionally, the caribou has provided horns for tools and implements, skin for clothing, and meat for food. The traditional winter parka made of caribou hide is essential. No quilted garment devised by white industry can give the same protection. Many tragic tales are told of the terrible years when the caribou did not come.

The incongruous scene above—an Inuit youth pedalling a bicycle across a frozen expanse of ice—is becoming more common in the Arctic as the native peoples adapt to white civilization.

Pond Inlet's setting is spectacular: a strip of civilization caught between icy slopes and frozen ocean, with the mountains of Bylot Island rising in the background. Visitors are warned not to try to walk across to Bylot, which, in the clear winter air, looks deceptively close. In spite of the illusion, it's actually a good fifteen miles away.

THE DENIAL OF WINTER

NOT LONG AGO IN THE CITY OF REGINA, A RADIO broadcaster remarked to me that this would be her last program for a fortnight. She, her husband, and their small children were about to embark on a February holiday. They could hardly wait to leave the snow-bound city for a warmer clime.

I asked her which Caribbean Island they were heading for—or had they chosen Hawaii, like so many other Westerners?

Her answer floored me: *Edmonton*, she told me. She was going to spend her two weeks' vacation in *Edmonton?* I once spent ten days there and the temperature never rose above minus fifty degrees Fahrenheit. I can think of no bleaker place in winter, with the possible exception of Aklavik. Why Edmonton?

She explained that she and the kids wouldn't be spending their holiday on the ski slopes or the toboggan runs. They'd be lying on an ersatz beach, lapped by arti-ficial waves, underneath potted palm trees, and when an adventurous whim struck them, they'd take an underwa-ter tour of a man-made lake in one of the several sub-marines available. In short, they were heading for the West Edmonton Mall, which has the advantage of being

a mere hour's flight away from their home in Regina.

Until the mall was built, Edmonton could scarcely be tabbed as the preferred destination for a winter holi-day. Now it has become a favourite resort city for a growing number of Canadians who want to pretend that winter doesn't exist.

It's no accident that the four Ghermezian brothers, who conceived the mall, hail from Iran, a land of hot sunshine, sand, and palm groves. Shopping centres, theme parks, and hotels were not new in Canada. It was the brothers' idea, however—a novel one—to put all of these under one roof and turn up the heat.

As Nader Ghermezian said when the third stage of the mall opened in September 1985, "it means you don't have to go to New York or Paris or Disneyland or Tampa or Hawaii. We have it all here for you in one place."

Jeffrey S.P. Hopkins, a McGill geographer, has pointed out that "we live in an era in which we can liter-ally select the time and place we want to experience." The West Edmonton Mall moves us one step closer to the virtual reality of the "holodeck" on the Starship *Enterprise*. Why go to Paris in the spring when a spanking

Prairie cities such as Calgary, Regina and Winnipeg, shown at left, link their buildings with covered walkways, fifteen feet above the street, so their citizens can escape the blasts of winter.

half.) Regina, Winnipeg, and Ottawa have followed with a combination of overhead walkways, glassed-in sidewalks, and tunnels.

And look what they've done to Portage and Main, traditionally the coldest and windiest intersection in Canada! The two streets are among the widest in the country, having grown out of the trails that had to accommodate Red River carts moving a dozen abreast. The winter wind fairly shrieks down these broad avenues. In spite of the weather—or perhaps because of it—Winnipeggers were proud of their historic corner, even boasting about the wind to visitors. The phrase "Portage and Main" stood as a kind of symbol for the ruggedness of the Canadian winter and, by inference, for the ruggedness of Canadians, especially Manitobans. Then, in 1959, the intersection was closed to pedestrians. The reason given wasn't the weather—it was traffic congestion. No doubt the planners also thought that shoppers using the tunnel beneath the streets would be grateful to escape the icy blasts above. Yet a good many people felt that the barricades must be temporary and that one day the intersection would again be opened to foot traffic. By 1993 a move was under way to restore Winnipeg's most popular gathering place to its earlier glory, in spite of the weather.

One problem with some subterranean cities is that people have trouble finding their way from one corridor to the other. This has been one of the problems afflicting Toronto's "empire of malls," as one social critic

Here, at the famous "windiest corner in Canada"—Portage and Main—shivering pedestrians huddle in the lee of Winnipeg's heritage buildings. To see how they escape across the intersection turn the page.

Winnipeg's notorious corner has had its winds tamed by an underground tunnel, complete with bas-relief, that protects pedestrians from the legendary winter.

called it. For years after the underground city was built, shoppers had no clear idea of where they were or where they were going. Were they under Richmond or King? How could they get out? Where was north, where was east? How could they move from one mall to another? There were few signs to tell them. Some people fantasized that there might have been a few lost souls trapped underground, unable to find their way out like rats in a maze, existing entirely on fast food, sleeping on furniture store settees, picking up fresh socks from a troglodyte haberdasher before trudging off on a fruitless search for an exit.

The reason for all this confusion was the individual landlords' attempts to persuade shoppers to spend their money where they were, rather than walk to another area. Fortunately for the human moles who wander blindly through this underground labyrinth, efforts were being made late in 1993 to bring some sort of order out of the chaos. Directional signs were now placed beneath the streets as well as above. The owners didn't like the term "underground," which suggested sewers, or perhaps a guerrilla movement, so they shunned the word. The new designation is *PATH: Toronto's Downtown Walkway.* "Follow PATH and you'll reach your downtown destination in weatherproof comfort," the slogan reads. It's the word "weatherproof" that attracts the customers. No need to tell them they're descending into the depths.

THE INDOOR SEASHORE

Winter has been banished at the West Edmonton Mall, where you can lie on a beach of trucked-in sand, and hear the machine-made waves lapping gently, and never ever venture out of doors into the cold until it's time to leave for the airport—just like any other vacationing tourist.

The West Edmonton Mall is humankind's ultimate response to nature. Its indoor lake is much more than a gigantic swimming pool, for here there are actual waves, a sandy beach, warm breezes, and even palm trees to diffuse the sunlight that creeps in through the cantilevered ceiling. Only in Canada, you say? So far. But where else in the Western world could four immigrant brothers have figured out a way of beating the cold, except in Canada's most northerly city?

In the world's biggest and most publicized shopping centre—eight city blocks long—you can do everything that people usually do on a winter holiday—dine and drink, sleep and frolic, and, if you have the stamina, patronize more than 800 shops. The West Edmonton Mall is a first for Canada, and there's little doubt that it will quickly spawn copies. It may be that this is the beginning of the ultimate "winter city," a community entirely covered by glass and centrally heated throughout.

WINTER IN DISGUISE

WHEN THE GREAT DEPRESSION HIT AND MY father was forced to take early retirement, we knew that we had experienced our last northern winter. It was too expensive to remain in the Yukon. Prices were sky high, especially in the dark days when nothing moved in or out of the territory. The cost of food and fuel alone would drain our savings account.

There was no argument about where we would settle. Victoria, the retiree's heaven, beckoned us as it did thousands of others fleeing the early frosts of Saskatchewan or the blizzards of Ontario. Victoria's frame houses required little insulation. Victoria's market gardens operated long after the prairies were unable to offer fresh produce.

For me it was a considerable culture shock—or, more correctly, a climatic shock—to wait for a winter that never arrived, at least not the kind of winter to which I'd been accustomed. On the Oak Bay links around the corner from our home, people played golf the year round. In fact, the CBC on its traditional cross-country Yuletide odyssey always ended up with people teeing off to the sound of Christmas church bells.

We had wallflowers still blooming in our garden on Christmas Day! In mid-February, the Japanese plum in our backyard burst into bloom. Some years it didn't snow at all. Now, we kids who had once longed for the day when the sun would return prayed for a blizzard that never came.

We shed our parkas forever. I was able to go with my Boy Scout troop on a hike every weekend of the year, bare-kneed in our traditional serge short pants. It often rained, but it was never very cold.

Then, as now, everybody on Vancouver Island seemed to be an amateur gardener—and no wonder. In North America, by one measurement, there are seven zones of hardiness based on weather statistics (I except Florida, which has two more). Regina and Winnipeg are in Zone One; Saint John and Calgary are in Zone Two; Toronto is in Zone Three, Chilliwack, B. C., in Zone Four, Vancouver in Zone Five. Only Victoria is in the mild Zone Six, which it shares with cities in New Mexico and Georgia.

That explains why certain trees and shrubs can survive a Canadian winter only in Victoria or on the islands that dot the Strait of Georgia. The arbutus or madrona

Almost every tourist who lands at Victoria heads for the Butchart Gardens (left) on the Saanich Peninsula, where, in a converted limestone quarry you can find blossoms year round. Here, in the foreground, the winter heather is in full bloom.

is one of these—a lovely, broad-leafed evergreen with a bright green trunk overlaid by peeling orange bark. The Garry oak is another. If you were spirited off in your sleep to awake in strange surroundings, the familiar gnarled shape of this unique and abundant tree would tell you at once where you were. It grows nowhere else in Canada.

Victoria revels in its slogan, "A Little Bit of Olde England," and works hard to preserve that image. The climate is certainly reminiscent of the old country. Indeed, it goes England one better. In the Köppen system of European weather classification, Victoria would be considered Mediterranean.

In my day, Victoria was *very* English. Women of a certain age appeared in Victorian hats and voluminous skirts. Old Territorials listed their military ranks in the telephone book and on plaques above their lych-gates. For a time, until they complained, the police were forced to wear helmets like English Bobbies. The Empress served a sumptuous English afternoon tea in its lobby (and still does), not to mention Indian curry, an Imperial dish that now has its own café, known as the Bengal Room. Ancient Brits tottered about town in pith helmets and khaki shorts, something they could not do in March in Toronto. And all because of the warm Japan current and the sheltering mountains that break the Pacific gales.

It is not only the English who flock to Victoria with its mock-Tudor half-timbers and its soft breezes. It is a mecca for all those who want the Canadian experience without the Canadian winter—everyone from tur-banned Sikhs to retired farmers, fed up with the white-outs of Manitoba and Saskatchewan. It is the image of Butchart Gardens, I think, that draws the retirees as well as the tourists. When the February blahs chill the bones, who can resist the image of a floral fairyland rising out of an abandoned stone quarry? There, the winter heather and jasmine, the daphne, and even the occasional English daisy are blooming beside the pansies and primroses. And in March, that vicious month when the snow still lies thickly over most of the country, the daffodils, hyacinths, and crocuses form beds of colour beneath the flowering fruit trees.

It is strange, in a book devoted to winter, to be writing about February flowers and Christmas without snow. Victoria belies the traditional image of Canada as a frozen wasteland. The soft rains of winter—so reminiscent of England—bear only a distant kinship to the howling blizzards that snarl traffic and shut down schools elsewhere in Canada. In more ways than one Victoria wears a disguise. The weather has made her unique, setting her off from the rest of the country. The weather has also brought a different kind of separatism. Ever since the days of the Carnarvon Club, which, in 1876, advocated total separation from the mainland, the city has cherished a small but vocal minority, some of whom would like to see their island return to the status of a British Crown colony. In my day the letters columns in the *Times* and *Colonist* abounded in such sentiments penned by Victorians who stoutly identified themselves as British to the core. We all thought they were a bit balmy, but then, so were the breezes.

LOTUS
LAND

By March—the worst month of the winter in much of Canada—the daffodils are blooming on Vancouver Island and the crocuses, snowdrops, and scilla are all but finished. Victoria has always been a city of gardeners; they have not only the climate, but many, being retired escapees from the snowbound prairies, have also the time.

Flowering trees provide an exotic background for the equally exotic totem poles in Thunderbird Park, Victoria. The totem poles themselves are an aspect of a climate so salubrious and a salmon economy so secure that tribal art flourished all year round. Thanks to the long season, a result in part of the warming effect of the Strait of Juan de Fuca (right), Victorians love to take to the water when they are not gardening or golfing. The links at Oak Bay (overleaf) were made famous by traditional CBC radio broadcasts, which featured men and women teeing off on Christmas Day.

In the land of the totem, winter comes in Technicolor, complete with mauve sunsets.

When February gives way to March, the daffodils are already being cut in Lotus Land at the largest daffodil farm in Canada—that of G.A. Vantreight and Sons on the Saanich Peninsula. The bulbs take up an entire 250 acres. Bulb farmers have brightened the Island for at least a hundred years. Now, the fourth generation of Vantreights has entered the business.

A Victoria winter is virtually devoid of snow, but not of wind.
The gale sweeps in from the Pacific, driving the ocean before it—hence the presence of sea walls and breakwaters.

In this verdant corner of the old Butchart quarry (left), there is little evidence of the stone that once was crushed to produce cement. Vines blur the rocky outlines, and a drift of spring daffodils heralds the end of Victoria's brief "winter."

FLIGHT FROM WINTER

WE ARE STRETCHED OUT ON THE BEACH IN Antigua, a family of Canadian escapees, sipping rum drinks from tall glasses and waiting for the newspapers to arrive so that we can gloat over the weather back home.

"I hope there's a blizzard blowing right now," one of my kids says.

"I hope they've closed Highway 401 because of drifting snow and black ice," says another.

"Maybe they've closed the schools," says my littlest daughter.

"There's no school, silly. It's the March break; everybody's come down here."

Everybody? It almost seems that way. In the bar and on the beach we encounter fellow Canadians who want to talk about the weather—not the cloudless skies of sunlit Antigua but the March winds that blow back home. They all hope for the worst.

The paper arrives and we seize it to check the temperature back in Toronto. Groans of disappointment! It's actually a few degrees above zero.

Every Canadian who goes south in the winter hopes in his or her heart that, through sheer luck or personal shrewdness, this refugee has escaped the worst storm of the season. The greatest disappointment of all is to arrive at Waikiki or Fort Lauderdale, only to learn that the weather has turned cold and wet, while the news from Canada enthuses over a succession of unusually clear and sunny days.

We all love the Canadian winter—even boast about it—when we're snorkelling off the beach at Roqueta Island, Acapulco, Mexico.

The world has shrunk since my youth. The jet planes and superhighways have transformed the tourist industry. Now, any Canadian who can scrape together enough to buy a package tour is able to enjoy June in January. In the first half of the century, this middle-class lifeline did not exist. We were like prisoners confined to a dark and chilly cell, reprieved at last and free to burst out into the sunlight. Now we have served our time. Oh blessed release!

In the old days, most of us had never seen a palm tree, except in the movies, though there were a few exceptions—hardy travellers with time on their hands, prepared to suffer long and often tedious journeys to reach their goal. In the summer of 1937, I worked with

An Air Nova connector plane leaves Halifax taking travellers to another heading for Florida. The weather is pretty bad: can the plane get away? All across Canada thousands of sun seekers chew their fingernails and hope against hope that they'll take off through the snow on time.

two of them, carpenters building bunkhouses for a mining company in the Yukon. This pair had only two topics of conversation: one was sex, the other was Tahiti (one subject, really).

In October, when the first snows fell and the work was done, these two would take their summer savings and head south. That meant a week-long steamboat trip to Whitehorse, followed by a journey over the Coast Mountains by train and a sea voyage down the Pacific coast to San Francisco. There they endured a long wait for a freighter that would take them to the enchanted islands, for there was no scheduled service. The journey from the Canadian North to the tropical South took at least a month and often much longer.

For them it was worth it—they escaped the winter. I envied them because they had filled my mind with visions of palm trees, white sands, sparkling waters, and, of course, the sensuous, brown-skinned girls. The following spring, with their money and their virility spent, they endured the long trip back to the Yukon and a seventy-hour workweek that stretched without a break until October, when they eagerly repeated the adventure.

There's now little doubt that the dark days of winter affect the human condition and that at least some of those who flee south are suffering from something more serious than the so-called February blahs. They go to Acapulco or Martinique to seek the light—the bright sunshine of the subtropics, so different from the gloom of a winter's day in Canada. A good deal of work has recently been done on the baffling condition known as SAD—Seasonal Affective Disorder—a deep depression suffered by some in the winter and alleviated only by repeated doses of bright light. People who suffer from SAD are clinically depressed. They gain weight, crave sweets, oversleep, withdraw socially, lose interest in sex, feel anxious, unstable, and listless. They act, in short, rather like a hibernating animal. The severity of affliction increases with distance from the equator. The disorder seems to be tied to absence or presence of light and is relieved by light therapy.

This may explain why, when people take their leave of Canada in its dark days, they talk, not so much about the warmth of the tropics, but of the presence of the sun. They speak of "seeking the sun," and much of the advertising for winter vacations emphasizes sunlight— Sunquest, or Suntours, to name two popular travel packages.

In my youth, only a few Canadians—like my two fellow workers—had the stamina or resources to escape the Canadian winter and see the sun. Air travel was in its infancy, highways were primitive, and the motel had yet to be invented. We stayed home and made the best of winter. Today half the population of my home town, Dawson City, flies off to Hawaii at the first hint of snow. Tahiti now has an airstrip that can handle jets. The only problem is that the palm groves are so full of Canadians, the girls who greeted my two co-workers are now in short supply.

The statistics of winter flight are awesome. One in

In Pearson's Terminal 3, a group of newly tanned travellers, returning to Toronto in shorts and flowered shirts, waits for the carousel to bring their baggage— grapefruit, no doubt, souvenirs, some half-empty bottles of suntan lotion, and with luck some warm clothing.

seven Canadians heads south every year to escape winter, at least temporarily. More than three hundred thousand western Canadians jet to Hawaii. A similar number flee to Arizona. Twice as many other Canadians seek refuge in the Caribbean. But the real mecca is Florida. Every winter almost two and a half million of us shake the snow from our boots, pack our swimsuits, and prepare for a vacation in Orlando, Fort Lauderdale, St. Petersburg, Key West, or points in between. Some stay no more than a week or two, but six hundred thousand wait out the winter in cottages or condos from November until April.

Florida is the paradise of choice partly because it is easily accessible—you can drive all the way, and half of all tourists do—and partly because, for most Canadians, there's no language barrier. And yet unilingual Quebeckers have also made it their home away from home. French Canadians are not noted for travelling, especially in their own country, but 650,000 leave La Belle Province each winter for the Sunshine State. They have, in fact, created a Petit Québec on the Atlantic coastal strip between Miami Beach and Fort Lauderdale. Like the Anglophones, they have their own newspapers and radio stations. The hotels and restaurants have learned the advantages of bilingualism. Les Québécois can follow the National Hockey League on cable TV, talk to a banker, lawyer, or accountant in their own tongue, and frolic in such night-spots as the aptly named Club Canadien.

Like Hawaii, Florida caters to Canadians of both languages because they bring money. The Canadian winter turns out to be hellishly expensive. The financial drain adds up to an annual $2.5 billion—the amount Canadians leave behind in the months of the Big Escape. In Toronto and Montreal in the peak winter months, the traffic thins out, the stores are half empty, and the restaurants become quiet as a lucrative chunk of the population departs for warmer climes or saves its money until it can afford to.

You can assess the dimensions of this annual flight by walking through any airport in the country, especially in February and March—the two months at season's end when Canadians feel they can no longer stand another ice storm. The terminal is a madhouse as the escapees crowd in, lugging suitcases crammed with everything from snorkel equipment to bottles of sunscreen. The lines at the ticket counters are prodigious. In the bars and lounges, it's standing room only.

Ghastly with the pallor of a long confinement, the sun seekers crowd into the departure lounges, shivering in the gaudy cottons that reveal their destinations. Meantime, more mobs pour off the planes and into the terminal buildings, sporting darkly tanned faces under incongruous straw hats, lugging packages of tax-free rum and net bags full of grapefruit in wistful memory of the days at the beach bar. Friends and relatives are there to greet them with obligatory remarks about how healthy and brown they look, and then to proffer, not without a certain smugness, the overcoats, furs, and parkas left in their care. Out they go into the Canadian night, bundled up to the nines, to face reality. Truly, there's no place quite like home.

THE COLOURS
OF WINTER

*When we think of winter, we tend to colour our imagination white, but
those who have leafed through this book have already experienced the navy
blue of a December afternoon in Dawson City, the purple twilight of a
Victoria evening, and the red and gold of a Manitoba dawn.
In the pictorial coda that follows, André Gallant's camera has captured the
vivid hues of our Canadian winter in all their infinite variety.*

WINTER

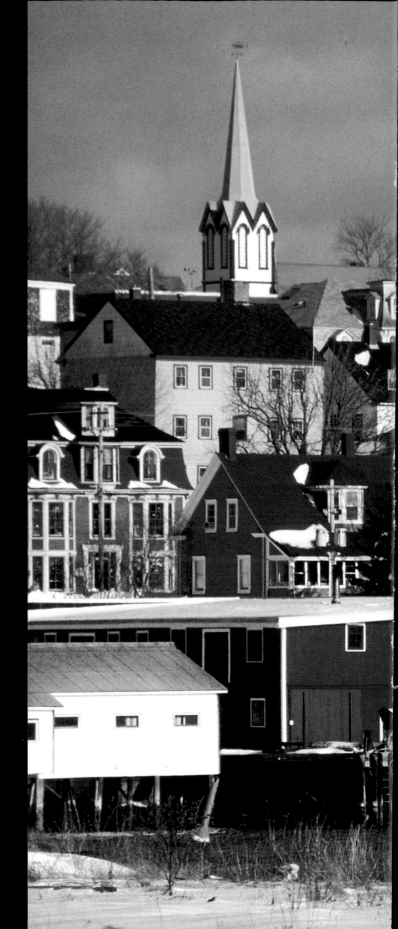